FOR MAX, BJÖRN, FREJ
& CHARLOTTE –
ROMAN RUIN EXPLORERS

Researched on location at Hadrian's Wall.
Historical consultant: Philip N Wood, Archaeologist.
Find out more about this book at
www.mickandbrita.com

No living creatures were harmed during the making of this book.

Roman Fort copyright © Frances Lincoln Limited 2004
Text and illustrations copyright © Mick Manning and Brita Granström 2004

First published in Great Britain in 2004 and in the USA in 2005 by
Frances Lincoln Children's Books, 74-77 White Lion Street,
London N1 9PF

www.franceslincoln.com

This edition published in Great Britain and in the USA in 2015

British Library Cataloguing in Publication Data available on request

ISBN 13: 978-1-84780-625-3

The illustrations are pencil and watercolour

Printed in China

1 3 5 7 9 8 6 4 2

ROMAN FORT

MICK MANNING & BRITA GRANSTRÖM

CONTENTS

FRANCES LINCOLN
CHILDREN'S BOOKS

WHO WERE THE ROMANS?

The Romans came from Italy and their capital city was Rome. They were clever people with new ideas about law, art, building and technology. With their mighty army and strong leaders, they invaded and conquered many countries and built a Roman Empire that would last from around 146 BC to AD 476. Some people welcomed Roman rule, but many fought against it until they were beaten by the Romans in battle.

Hadrian's Wall in northern England and the Raetien border in Germany are two famous frontiers and they form part of a network of forts and towns that covered the whole Roman Empire. The Romans had well-organized supply lines, and the people who lived under Roman rule had to provide money, food, gold, silver and slaves. Roman armies were stationed all over the frontier to make sure they did!

The ROMAN EMPIRE

BRITAIN

GERMANY

FRANCE

ITALY

Rome

SPAIN

GREECE

TURKEY

SYRIA

EGYPT

NORTH AFRICA

OUR FORT

The Roman fort in this sketchbook is on the northern frontier, far away from the city of Rome. Let's meet some of the people and look in on their lives.

Vespian
a centurion

Flavinus
a standard bearer

Candidus
a decurion

Felix
the fort commander

Claudia and Max
Felix's wife and their son

Lepidina and Titus
Claudia's best friend and her son

Marcus
a slave

Emperor Severus
the ruler of the Empire

Queen Meg
a local Celtic queen

Claudia is having a birthday party and she has invited her best friend Lepidina. But Lepidina lives twenty dangerous miles away so Vespian has been sent to bring her safely to the fort...

It's raining cats and dogs!

Listen! Jangle, tramp! Jangle, tramp!
As the soldiers march, the sound of their metal
belts mixes with the tramp of their studded boots.

Lepidina and Claudia write to each other
but haven't met for months. 20 miles is
a long way to travel in this wild country...

• A centurion like Vespian was in charge of a unit of 80 men called a century.

• Each century had a second-in-command called an optio, a trumpeter and standard bearers. Six centuries made a cohort and often included cavalry.

Flavinus, the standard bearer, holds the standard high.

Vespian is leading the troop back to the fort. On the way he must visit a powerful queen.

Flavinus also looks after his century's wages.

ON PATROL

Vespian's patrol is escorting Lepidina over the mountains. Roman troops must keep the Empire in order, even here in this rainy place somewhere on the northern frontier.

• A 2000-year-old party invitation from a Roman lady called Claudia is the earliest surviving example of women's handwriting.

• Written with ink on birchwood, it was one of many letters dug up in the ruins of Vindolanda, a Roman fort in Northumberland, England.

WARRIOR QUEEN

Meg is a powerful Celtic queen. Some Celts still hate the Romans but Meg realised long ago that trade with the Empire could make her tribe rich. Vespian has a nickname for her – The Wild Cat!

Celtic houses are made of stones or woven branches covered with mud. The roofs are thatched with grass or reeds.

Enemy heads on poles to bring good luck!

The queen's daughters are full of mischief!

• The Celtic people of the northern frontiers lived in small villages. Each village was part of a larger tribe with its own king or queen.

• The Romans called the tribes 'barbarians' but the Celts made beautiful jewellery and used money, soap and perfume.

ide it's smoky and dark – but very cosy!

The queen has never seen a peacock before! She is giving Vespian a puppy in return.

Sharp sticks are used to guard the village.

He smells of soap

Bleached hair

Tattoos and plant dye body paint

warm clothes in bright colours

He smells of ferrets!

'Arrow' will soon grow into a fast, hairy hunting dog.

• To keep the peace, the Romans darked and gave many gifts from their Empire, including fine pottery, silver and peacocks.

• A famous Celtic queen called Boudicca burned London and massacred hundreds of people in revenge for attacks on her own family by Roman soldiers.

oxen bring stone from the quarry.

'Creak' go the oxcart wheels.

milestones mark distances between places.

Assistants hold up markerpoles to Quintus.

"It's sweaty work."

Some soldiers work - others stand guard.

The road is higher in the middle so any rain runs off into the ditches to avoid flooding.

• Romans used metal shovels, just like the ones you can find today in any hardware store.

• Roman engineers also built bridges and aqueducts. A fine example of a Roman aqueduct is at Pont Du Gard in France.

ROAD BUILDERS

Vespian's patrol has met up with Quintus and his road builders. Quintus loves building straight roads. The army can march quickly and easily from place to place, making it safer for everyone.

stubborn mules carry things too!

Quintus the surveyor decides which way the road should go. He plots the road across the countryside using an instrument called a 'groma'.

The Roman Road Recipe:
① Dig a deep trench
② Fill it with broken stone and sand well packed down
③ Lay cobbles, paving stones or gravel on top.

What's that far-away sound? strange trumpets... coming closer

• By mixing broken tiles and small stones with cement, Romans made strong concrete. Concrete is still used by modern builders!

• Roads were kept as straight as possible but they did bend around burial grounds and holy places because the Romans were superstitious.

Loud signals are blown on the trumpet.

Look at the way Vespian gives orders.

Celtic horn shaped like a wild boar.

People shout!
people scream!
Warhorns honk! Dogs bark!

The cavalry spreads panic amongst the enemy.

Candidus the decurion saves the day.

• Skeletons of Celts and Romans have been found showing tell-tale signs of battle injuries.

• Romans could stitch wounds, mend broken bones and even do amputations. But sickness and infection were the biggest killers.

AMBUSH!

This ambush could have led to disaster for
Lepidina. Vespian's men are outnumbered.
Luckily Candidus rides to the rescue.
What a hero! Celtic prisoners will face death,
slavery or life as Roman soldiers.

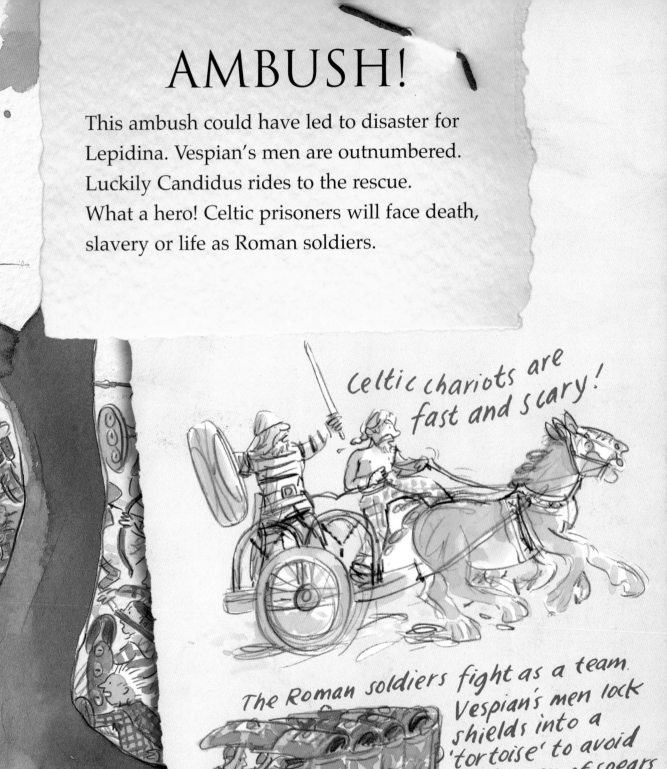

Celtic chariots are fast and scary!

The Roman soldiers fight as a team. Vespian's men lock shields into a 'tortoise' to avoid a shower of spears and arrows.

• The Roman army was not always victorious.
In AD 9 three whole legions were wiped out
by fierce German tribes.

• Celts fought with spears, slingshots, bows and swords.
They had fast war chariots too.

AT THE FORT

Max likes to climb the hill. He can see the whole fort from up here: soldiers on parade, supplies arriving and being unloaded. Max's home is a very busy place!

Prisoners from the ambush ↓

Vespian's patrol is giving the password to open the gate

The headquarters is the nerve centre of the fort. The offices, strongroom and regiment flags and trophies are kept here.

The fort commander's house is large and even has a garden and private bathroom.

A watch-tower

The granary can hold enough food to feed 500 people for many months.

Max is waving to Vespian's patrol. He will see his friend Titus soon. It's windy today!

• Roman forts were built in the same shape as a playing card, with round corners. The very first forts were made of wood but later they were built of stone.

• The granary was where grain and other food supplies were stored. It was built on stilts to allow fresh air to circulate and to keep out the mice.

West gate

Fort commander's house

Headquarters

Hospital

Granary and food store

vespian's quarters

cavalry patrol

vicus or settlement

Bar

shops

Bath house

• Centurions and decurions had their own quarters at the end of each barrack block. The cavalry soldiers often shared with their horses!

• The main gate's stone doorsteps were heavily worn by iron cartwheels. These deep ruts still exist today at many Roman fort ruins.

Rebels prefer life as a soldier to slavery - who wouldn't?

"You pay for your own kit so look after it!"

"Haircut"

"Sign up for a life in the army."

Too small?

Too big!

"chain-mail is heavy but it can save your life!"

The senior centurion growls at the new recruits...

"You'll earn a good pay now that Rome is your mother. But you must learn to fight like a Roman too."

There are two sorts of Roman soldiers. Vespian's legionaries are Roman citizens but tribesmen who volunteer usually join as auxiliaries

• Medics, clerks, musicians and craftsmen were excused from the boring jobs the soldiers had to do – things like cleaning the bath house or polishing armour.

• The soldiers' daily ration of food was about 1½ kgs (3 lbs) of bread, 1 kg (2¼ lbs) of meat, 1 litre (4½ cups) of wine and 400 millilitres (1½ cups) of olive oil.

A SOLDIER'S LIFE

A Roman soldier's life is always hard: miles of marching, hours of guard duty, drill, sword practice and sometimes battles. If the new recruits think that's tough, wait until they meet the senior centurion!

pilum

'gladius' sword

shield

leather sandals with iron studs

helmet and bedroll

wooden chest

Pots and pans.

drying socks

8 soldiers in a room

bunk beds

vespian's sweaty men are hungry after their march.

digging tools

sore feet from marching.

sore eyes from the smoke in here!

They cook together in their room.

• A soldier's life was tough. Deserters could be badly beaten, or even stoned to death.

• Soldiers usually joined the army for 20 years but about half of all recruits didn't survive long enough to retire.

People have scratched silly poems and drawings on the plaster walls.

The water flows under here floating the POO away.

This is what it looks like under the floor.

• The Romans were clever plumbers – they even used lead water pipes.

• Infection and disease were common. Many Romans had roundworms from drinking dirty water and eye infections from smoky fires.

ON THE TOILET

Fresh water flows in here.

Going to a Roman toilet is a time for a chat – no one is embarrassed or shy. A short roof keeps the rain off the seats but allows fresh air in. Running water trickles along the floor. Candidus, Vespian and Flavinus are planning an off-duty trip into town.

Sponges on sticks to wipe your bum. You wash your sponge stick and put it back for someone else to use!

It's really smelly in here!

Lots of flies

There is a stone trough to wash your hands – but no soap!

Next stop the bath house, the best place to be on a cold day like this!

• A typical Roman toilet could seat many people at a time.

• It is possible that sponges may have been soaked in vinegar as a sort of disinfectant.

THE BATH HOUSE

The soldiers' bath house is a lovely building. It has decorated plaster walls and cold plunge pools. It has warm baths and steamy sauna rooms. It even has a changing room with board games and music – what a nice way to relax on the northern frontier!

Candidus has been on cavalry patrol for three days. He stinks like a sweaty horse!

Marcus

olive oil

Voices chatting and laughing... the clacking of board games

A statue of **FORTUNA**. The Roman goddess of good luck.

Romans use olive oil instead of soap. They scrape off the muck with a metal scraper called a **strigil**.

who do you think is winning?

• The bath houses and the commander's quarters were kept warm with an under-floor heating system called a hypocaust.

• Warm air from a special fire circulated under the stone floors and warmed the rooms.

It takes a lot of wood to heat the bath house.

A slave stokes the fire.

Vespian is telling Flavinus about his new puppy.

wooden sandals

Beautiful mosaic pattern

• Some floors got so hot that people had to wear wooden shoes to protect their feet.

• Hollow clay bricks in the walls let the warm air circulate. The windows were double-glazed too!

Bar - Rosie sells drinks and tasty hot and cold snacks.

• The settlements that grew up around every frontier fort attracted people from all over the Roman Empire.

• There were butchers, dressmakers, street musicians, magic charm sellers, wives and mothers. Retired soldiers often stayed too, opening up shops or bars.

Landlady- Mara rents out rooms to the soldiers' secret wives. She makes a lot of money.

Claudia's slave is buying all the food for the household.

Baker- Catty is a local girl. She and her daughter sell freshly baked bread.

Fishseller- Ostia has followed her sons here from far away. Her boys are both in the army.

olive stones and Roman coins.

THE — — SETTLEMENT

Over the years, a large settlement has grown outside the fort. It is where traders, shopkeepers and landladies gather to make a living from the soldiers' wages.

• Only officers were allowed to marry but many soldiers had secret wives living in the settlement.

• Roman cafes opened out on to the street, selling 'fast food' like olives, honey cakes, black pudding, meatballs and barley soup. Drinks included beer and wine.

Roman Toothpaste Recipe:
Powdered horn
Ground up oyster shells
Ashes of dogs' teeth
Mixed up with honey!

Lepidina has linen underwear.

Only important Romans like Felix can wear a toga

Roman children wear a lucky charm called a 'Bulla'.

slaves like Marcus do all the work.

cotton underpants

It's hard to lace your own sandals when you're 3 years old.

• Slaves did all the work. A slave could belong to a rich owner or be shared among a group of rough soldiers. Slaves could be house-pets or worked to death!

• To keep their legs smooth and silky, Roman women used a cream made of goat's blood, mixed with sea palm and powdered snake!

DRESSING UP

Everyone is getting ready for the birthday party. The slaves are working very hard. Claudia and Lepidina take fashion very seriously. Even here, on the rainy frontier, they have copied the latest hairstyles by looking at coins and statues brought from Rome.

Roman ladies' slaves are always well dressed.

Claudia's hair smells of perfumed oil.

Lovely polished metal mirror

Expensive make-up comes in glass jars.

Ochre on lips

chalk on neck

Silk shawl from Rome

• Foundation cream was made from dirt and sweat from sheep's wool. Mascara was made from bear fat and soot!

• Romans used bird droppings and honey to get rid of spots.

27

PARTY

Claudia's birthday party is in the commander's quarters – the best rooms in the fort. With musicians, dancers and a magnificent feast, the celebrations will go on late into the night.

A slave goes round with a pot in case anyone needs a wee – Ugh!

A slave brings a piglet.

Musicians play while a slave dances.

Everyone eats with their fingers.

Oil lamps light the room.

Boar's head, deer meat and chicken... Peacock eggs and fruit.

• A Roman party trick was to put live birds in a roast boar. They flew out when it was cut open.

• Snails were fattened up by feeding them milk or meat.

There is local beer too. Lots of **burping!**

Lepidina loves chicken and raw oysters.

chicken leg

Everyone including the children drinks watered-down wine.

Roman children love honey cakes!

Garlic-buttered snails.

bread

beautiful glass jug

Dormice pie!

quail eggs

Some people are sick outside so they can eat some more.

• Dormice were kept in special cages and fed on nuts and acorns.

• Slaves waited on the guests and washed their fingers between meals.

ROMAN CHILDREN

Only the officers can afford a teacher at the fort. On this cold morning the boys are studying mathematics and learning that the world is flat! Girls are taught reading, writing, cooking, music and needlework at home.

Boys have to learn things 'word-for-word' – this teacher beats them with a stick if they don't remember!

statue of a famous poet

Greeks make good teachers. Max's teacher is an ex-slave.

The boys write with styli on wax tablets.

MAX

Abacus for doing sums

• Slaves could sometimes be freed as a reward for faithful service. Well-educated freed slaves often took jobs as clerks or teachers.

• Rich Romans could read and write but slaves and poor people got no education at all.

Flora likes rolling a hoop.

Titus plays with his toy chariot.

Helena is painfully out of tune. Ouch!

All boys like to play fight with wooden swords.

Balls are made from leather.

Max is clever at stick and ball games.

Emperor Severus is giving Candidus a crown of oak leaves for rescuing Lepidina and Titus from the ambush. This is a great honour.

THE EMPEROR

The emperor has arrived with his wife and children. They have travelled thousands of bumpy Roman miles on a tour of their frontier. The local arena is putting on a show with two famous gladiators, Paxos and Thrax.

The guard of honour wear ceremonial masks made of silver.

oak leaves

• Some emperors were cruel and selfish. Others were wise. Hadrian built Hadrian's Wall and Marcus Aurelius wrote a famous book called *Meditations*.

• The most famous arena in the world was the Colosseum in Rome, but small arenas were built all over the Empire.

BOO! Hurrah! Boo! hiss! OOh!

She fights with a net and a trident.

He fights with a sword.

Thrax and Paxos don't fight to the death – they are too valuable! Their pretend fight is all part of the show and the crowds LOVE IT!

Paxos and Thrax give souvenirs to their fans.

• At the Colosseum, unarmed prisoners were often fed to hungry lions to entertain the crowds.

• Most gladiators fought to the death and usually survived for only 2 or 3 fights.

Rosie nails a curse tablet to the temple wall. She is asking the gods to punish a thief!

Outside the temple, Felix is sacrificin a boar. He will burn the heart and th liver as offerings to Mars, god of w so his soldiers will have success in battle.

Jupiter - the king of the Roman gods...

Juno - his queen

Neptune - god of the sea

Venus - goddess of love.

Diana - goddess of the moon

Apollo - god of the sun.

Claudia's household shrine - Max leaves food as an offering to the family spirits that protect the

• Little models of legs or ears made of clay or lead were left at temples to beg the gods to help heal injuries.

• All Roman families had a household shrine. The small figures represent family spirits who protect the home.

ROMAN GODS

It's dusk at the fort and all is well. The Roman gods are being worshipped tonight in this rainy place, somewhere on the northern frontier.

moths come to the light.

Vespian is wearing a raven mask.

The sweet scent of a burning pinecone fills the dark room.

Flavinus is wearing a lion head mask.

This is a secret ceremony held for Mithras, Lord of Light.

• Jupiter was father to a large family of Roman gods. His thunderbolt and eagle were the badges of Rome.

• Although gods from other religions were worshipped, Christianity wasn't popular because it didn't use sacrifices. That upset Jupiter and the emperor!

Bad news has just come in...

The frontier tribes are preparing for war!

END OF THE EMPIRE

The Roman Empire lasted hundreds of years and became Christian in AD 320. Emperor Constantine split the Empire into two, ruling the eastern part of the Empire from Constantinople in Turkey. When the western part was invaded by Germanic tribes, the legions were called home to defend Rome. But Rome was destroyed in AD 410 and the people of its once great Empire were left undefended. Many would soon face new invaders: the Saxons from Germany and the Jutes from Denmark.

WHAT THE ROMANS LEFT BEHIND . . .

Latin is still taught today and is at the heart of many modern languages like Italian and Spanish. Many Latin words exist in English, German and French too. We still use Roman letters and all the months still have Roman names. For example, March is named after Mars and June after the goddess Juno. Archaeologists have excavated buildings all over the Roman Empire, finding statues, weapons, tools, writing tablets and personal possessions. Many Roman ruins are open to visitors so why not explore a Roman fort yourself one day?

ABACUS – page 30.
A simple counting device made of wooden beads on a metal frame.
ARENA – pages 32 & 33.
A circular Roman 'sports stadium' where chariot racing, battles between gladiators and wild animal fighting could be watched.
AUXILIARIES – page 18.
Soldiers who fought for the Roman army from all corners of the Empire but who were not Roman citizens. Prisoners of war often chose to be soldiers instead of slaves.
CELTS – pages 10, 11, 14, 15 & 31.
The tribes of people living in Britain and south of Europe at the time.
CENTURY – page 8.
A unit of 80 men with its own barrack block.
CENTURION – pages 8 & 18.
An officer in charge of a century. Many started out as ordinary soldiers and so had lots of experience.
CHAIN MAIL – page 18.
Small links of iron made into a vest and worn for protection in battle.
COHORT – page 8.
An army unit made up of centuries. Usually between 500 and 1000 soldiers.
CROWN OF OAK LEAVES – page 32.
A special award given to a soldier or unit for rescuing a Roman citizen. This was also called a civica.
CURSE TABLET – page 34.
People wrote curses asking the gods to give their enemies bad luck. They left them at temples or buried them in the ground.
DECURION – page 14.
A cavalry officer.
DESERTER – page 19.
A soldier that runs away from the army.
EMPEROR – page 32 & 36.
The ruler of the Roman Empire. Rome wasn't always ruled by emperors. For hundreds of years it was ruled by a government called a Republic.
EMPIRE – pages 6, 9, 10, 11, 24 & 36.
Lands belonging to another country that have been taken in battle or invaded.

The Headquarters building is buzzing like a wasp's nest!

Vespian is doubling the guard.

GLOSSARY & INDEX

Have you read the other Fly On The Wall books?

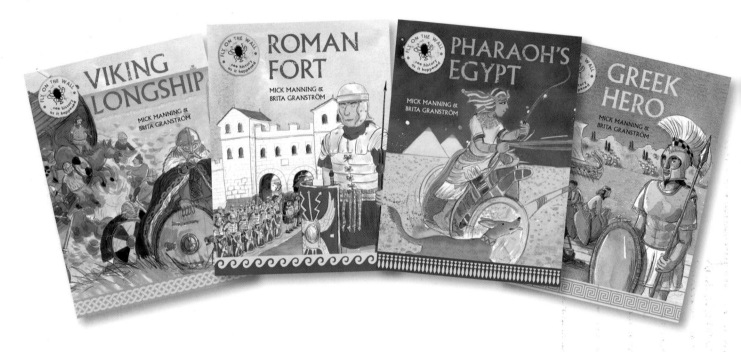

See how the mummy-makers perform their grisly work and sail down the Nile in *Pharaoh's Egypt*. Patrol with a windswept centurion, eavesdrop in the smelly toilets and dine at a tasty banquet in *Roman Fort*. Watch skilful ship builders at work, visit a Viking farmstead and charge into battle in *Viking Longship*, and follow a Greek soldier to the Olympics in *Greek Hero*.

These books are packed with up-to-date information, detailed drawings and colourful characters, so you can be a fly on the wall and see history as it happened!

'The sketchbook format has an energy and warmth which really brings history to life.' – *Books for Keeps*

'This book and others in the series deserve to be placed with the best history books for young learners.' – *English Association Magazine* on *Greek Hero*